New World Pilgrimage

"Walk The Earth"
(First Edition)

By:
Johnny Brando

Dedication

"Friends are as companions on a journey, who ought to aid each other to persevere in the road to a happier life."
- Pythagoras

I dedicate this book to the future and the

future generations. May it help you find

the peace, serenity and the life that you

have been thirsting for.

Table of Contents

Introduction

"A journey of a thousand miles begins with a single step." Lao Tze - *The Way of Lao-tzu Chinese philosopher (604 BC - 531 BC)*

What is a pilgrimage you may wonder? It is essentially a trip or a journey that is focused on the quest for spiritual or moral significance. Oftentimes, it is a trip to a certain location of significance to an individual's faith and belief, like a shrine; however, most of the time the journey can be metaphorical to an individual's belief. A lot of religions—all over the world—ascribe spiritual significance to certain places, such as:

- Sites that are believed to have special spiritual powers;

- places where a divine being is "housed" or said to be living;
- sites where miracles have been seen or performed;
- places where divine beings had their spiritual awakening or calling;
- places where a deity or deities have either a verbal or visual connection with God; or
- The locations of death or birth of saints or founders of the religion.

These places are venerated with either temples or shrines that believers are urged to visit for their spiritual advantage like finding answers to questions, spiritual healing and many other spiritual benefits.

The person who goes on such a journey is known as a pilgrim.

Religions & Pilgrimage

Going on a pilgrimage is highly associated with a person's religion. And we will have a brief insight into each religion who encourage their followers to embark on a pilgrimage

Bahá'í Faith

The Bahá'í Faith is focused on three core principles:

- The unity of God – that there is only one God who is the sources of all creation;
- The Unity of Religion – that all major religions have the same spiritual source and come from the same God; and

- The Unity of Humanity – that all humans have been created equal and that the diversity of race and culture are seen as worthy of appreciation and acceptance.

The Bahá'í pilgrimage involves visiting the holy places found in Haifa, Akká and Bahji at the Bahá'í World Trade Center located in Northwest Israel. This is a nine-day pilgrimage where specific rites are prescribed. Each Bahá'í Faith follower is urged to go on a pilgrimage to any one of this site so long as he or she can afford it, is able to do so and that no obstacles stand in their way.

Buddhism

Buddhism is a form of religion that does not depend on the presence of Gods. Buddhism embraces a wide array of practices, beliefs and traditions that are mostly based on the teachings of Siddhartha Gautama—also known as the 'awakened one' or Buddha.

In Buddhist pilgrimage, there are basically 4 focal sites worthy of pilgrimage for the Buddhists that would produce a feeling of spiritual urgency:

- Kusinara – This is the place where Buddha died which is now known as Kushinagar, Uttar Pradesh, India.
- Sarnath – This is the place where Buddha first delivered his first teaching and is formally known as Isipathana.

- Bodh Gaya – This is the location of Buddha's enlightenment where the current Mahabodhi Temple is situated.
- Lumbini – This is Buddha's birthplace located in Nepal.

However, with the globalization of the Buddhism, there are already numerous famous places for Buddhist pilgrimage in different countries of the world. Here are some places to name a few:

- The City of Ten Thousand Buddhas – located in California USA.
- Three Jewel Temples – located in Bulguska, South Korea.
- Kansai Kannon Pilgrimage and Shikoku Pilgrimage – located in Nara and Kyoto, Japan.

- The Bamiyan Buddhas – located in Afghanistan.

Christianity

Christianity is the host for other sub-religions that believe in one God—Jesus Christ. The Christian-based religions are grounded upon the oral teachings and life of Jesus Christ as offered in the New Testament.

Most Christian pilgrimages are made to visit the places that are associated with the resurrection, crucifixion, life and birth of their God, Jesus Christ. However, these pilgrimages are not only for God but also to places that are related and important to apparitions of the Virgin Mary, Christian martyrs, saints, or apostles.

Hinduism

Hinduism is best described as a categorization of distinct philosophical or intellectual points of view rather than a rigid set of beliefs. Its beliefs and teachings comprises of societal norms, dharma, karma, shaktism, Vaishnavism, shaivism and many other traditions.

The places in Hinduism pilgrimages are related to epic events in the lives of many gods; most of the time this places are sacred mountains, lakes, rivers and cities. All Hindus are urged to partake on a pilgrimage but it is not mandatory and most who go on a pilgrimage visit the sites that are found within their region.

Islam

Islam is a monotheistic religion that strictly adheres to the verbatim word of Allāh as articulated in the Qur'an.

In Islam, the pilgrimage of Mecca is the important pilgrimages in the religion and should be embarked on by any able bodied Muslim even once in their life. The pilgrimage to Mecca is one of the five Pillars of Islam, which further cements its importance in the religion.

Judaism

Judaism is a monotheistic religion based on the Hebrew Bible known as Torrah. Judaism is basically the way of life, philosophy and religion of the Jewish people—it is the expression of the covenantal relationship that God has established with the children of Israel.

In Judaism, there are three pilgrimage festivals of Sukkot, Shavuot and Passover which is currently located in the Wailing wall, Western wall or Temple Mount. There are many other pilgrimage sites scattered all throughout the world.

Zoroastrianism

This is an ancient Iranian religion brought about by the teachings of Zoroaster. The religion believes that there is one supreme, transcendent and universal go the wise lord or Ahura Mazda.

In Zoroastrianism there are several pilgrimage sites that are known as pirs that can be found in several provinces but the most famous of which is in the province of Yazdi. Most of these pilgrimage sites are ancient fire temples and its remains.

Final Thoughts

As you can see, since time immemorial, pilgrimages have been done by people of the faith. In time, you will better understand the importance of knowing what pilgrimage is, side by side the meaning and depth of the New World Pilgrimage.

~ o ~

Chapter 1: The New World Pilgrimage

You might be under the impression that the New World Pilgrimage, or NWP for short, is a form of a new religion—but, I will answer you in a straightforward manner that it is NOT.

What is the New World Pilgrimage?

Why? Because NWP it is a new way of life that I am revealing to you. I am not offering you a new GOD—you are free to choose the God that you want to serve and worship. You are also free not to worship God. This is why the answer is a no—New World pilgrimage is not a religion.

However, New World Pilgrimage is a geo-political movement—is a new way of life.

So, to rephrase my answer again that NWP not a religion, it is accurate to say New World Pilgrimage is new system of world government based on a new form of exchange, but not a religion.

Though NWP is not a religion note that New World Pilgrimage will enhance the better side of all the religions of the world because the new world is open to all people and all kinds of faiths. It allows everyone to believe and express their religious or even non-religious beliefs openly and freely. After all without religious freedom you really don't have freedom.

America for example was established through the pursuit of religious freedom in the new world. If you can't worship that which is unseen and intangible then how are you going to have freedom within a world which is visible? Religion is the seed of all Freedom. The idea of worldwide pilgrimage is to create an environment that allows more time to pursue both the natural world and the greater portion of reality which is the unseen. New World Pilgrimage allows people to believe, express, and change their beliefs without being dependent on Nations, Communities, and Families because their food, shelter, and clothing are provided for by the support system. This allows people to live without having to submit to the ways of nation, culture, or even Family.

Borderless World

In essence, New World Pilgrimage is about walking around the whole planet at least once in your lifetime. One of the main objective is the elimination of all borders. Walking is the great mediator and catalyst that can expand and simplify all things in the new world. Imagine a new world economy that works completely on the concept of travel. Through a new exchange of service you will eventually earn your citizenship to a new nomadic world.

In the past people were unable to communicate great distances due to lack of technology, the existence of boundaries that were the natural result of language. Today with the advancement of communication mass numbers of people can be coordinated around the globe to rid the planet of those who want to keep us enslaved to possessions and property. The old systems of that we still live in today can be eliminated creating a free world for the people and by the people. With the recent global capability of our times it is now possible to expand the great concepts of freedom for a journey of a lifetime.

Freedom

Not all people are free to walk the earth. In a deeper sense very few are free and they only know crude forms of freedom. In a more real sense many people around the world are not allowed to travel to other place due to national borders. Though these borders can about as the result of protecting the people of a certain region of the world this is no longer necessary. New World Pilgrimage will make it possible for all people of the world to make the journey in the most efficient way possible. With the simultaneous removal of all boarders around the world.

When all possessions and national borders are eliminated in every corner of the world people will walk around the whole planet on foot and help others to do the same. This is more than monumental... This is for the greater good of all people.

It would also important to note: that which has value will be apparent to the new walking society and the rest discarded. The nomadic life creates its own culture and even subcultures based on the soul idea of making it around the planet and the freedom of mind this creates.

Open Source

Yes, you read it right. New World Pilgrimage is an open source idea, which means that people can add to the idea, modify it to make it better. Streamlining the whole process.

Just like with any open source system, NWP works this way. Let's take a look at samples of Open Source and I am sure you have heard of Wikipedia. Wikipedia is a best known example for an open source system. It's people like you and me who made it what it is today. Its people like you and me, along with experts, researchers, entertainers and many others who add up to the growing information on each of Wikipedia's pages. Wikipedia was not built and finished in a day. In fact, it's still evolving into a great resource—people are still adding information into it. And if you don't know it already, Wikipedia was not made by a single person nor a group of people—it is made by people all over the world with the common goal of spreading information or having a database of information that any person in the world can access for free. That is what open source is all about.

As Wikipedia has said, open source is "any system of innovation or production that relies on goal-oriented yet loosely coordinated participants, who interact in order to create a product (or service) of economic value, which they make available to contributors and non-contributors alike." Simply put, open source is open collaboration from people of all walks of life. Infuse this concept with the idea of walking across the planet on foot with a fully engaged support system and you then have something special.

The 5 Pillars of NWP

The five pillars for all individuals in the New World Of Pilgrimage are:

1) **No possessions** – In the New World Pilgrimage the Pillar of No Possessions entails the avoidance of associated evils. Which are the pursuit of an object, securing an object, supplying an object, and maintaining an object.

2) **No property** – In the New World Pilgrimage the Pillar of No property entails the avoidance of associated evils which are the pursuit of a property, securing property, building property, and maintaining a property.

3) **No money** - In the New World of Pilgrimage the Pillar of No property and

possessions entails the avoidance of associated evils which are the creation of money and/or the need for currency.

4) **No borders** – In the New World Pilgrimage, you must earn your citizenship to the new nomadic world of pilgrimage; a borderless world free to all people of the earth. With no borders to keep people in one place. Walking the planet will transform all people and dissolve old cultures into a new nomadic world culture.

5) **No competition** – In the New World Pilgrimage, there is no competition because competition breeds evil. Without competition, people will be more contented with their life.

The 3-Fold Treasure

In NWP, it has three postulates on treasure and these are:

1) Walking around the surface of planet earth.
2) Helping others do the same.
3) Earning citizenship to the new nomadic world

Further, When looking at the world I do it from 3 levels of thought that are separate and yet linked by a common thread. They are held in this order. The higher levels cancel out the lower levels. This formula will help people understand New World Pilgrimage.

1) The Eternal
2) The World
3) The National

With the evil of the "national" gone, you only have the "world" for the body and the "eternal" for the soul. Just as the world cancels out the national, when we leave the body the eternal will ultimately cancel out the world. This is pure reason.

How Do You Become Part of the NWP?

In New World Pilgrimage you must earn your citizenship to the new world. Citizenship is not a birthright. You must earn it through stages. This means that while you are young you need to stay within way stations for development and later work. First you have to be educated in the manner that NWP deems proper and fitting to be able to continue the cycle of this walking culture (you will learn more in in-depth on how the education system of NWP is going to be pursued in the succeeding chapters).

Once you have been schooled, it is now time for you to apply this knowledge firsthand, like doing agriculture, setting up water sources along the way, providing or creating shelter to those who are already a citizen of NWP and have made their way to your station on the route to replenish their supply. Once you graduate from this stage, you are now a full-fledged New World Pilgrimage citizen. While completing a full circumnavigation of the earth you will become an elder that affords extra decision-making rights in the new nomadic world society within the framework of the 5 pillars and 3 fold treasure of New World Pilgrimage.

Think in terms of living a nomadic life of walking around the planet, mass migrations of people, and the one world support system that allows it all to happen.

Once established, there will be way-stations one day's journey in every direction for food, shelter, clothing, and water along all worldwide routes. A new world exchange (economy) based on walking the planet on foot will be in place.

Let no national border hold you back from walking the planet. The world will be yours to walk. The New World Pilgrimage will open new frontiers of faith for all peoples, but not limited to faith. People will no longer be confined to cultural prejudices.

The subject of intolerance is only one of many international topics that New World Pilgrimage is more than capable of solving.

Final Thoughts

Is New World Pilgrimage something that should be kept secret from the world? To keep only for oneself? NO! It's something for the whole world to know about and eventually live.

~ o ~

Chapter 2: Science - The Great Hope.

The New World Pilgrimage is a movement that is unlike any other. It encourages people to walk this earth so that they may gain wisdom and learn new ways on how we should live our lives as responsible and accountable human beings. Since we become more accountable, the New World Pilgrimage gives natural hope to all mankind. So how do we restore hope in humanity with the New World Pilgrimage? Basically, one of the by-products of walking on foot will help us cultivate both individual and collective creativity leading to fulfilling the 3 basic needs of food, shelter, and clothing. Read on.

Learning How to Think

We live in the comforts and conveniences that our society provides for us to the extent that we abuse our environment. The creation of cars, offshore drilling facilities, and nuclear energy plants may provide us with comfortable living now, but is it good for us? The thing is that we never learn despite that these type technologies among many other are robbing us of a good clean Earth.

To make matters worse, technologies and the ideas that rise forth from them also gives us a linear track of mind that produces the unnecessary. It seems that everyone thinks the same even if we look different. We share the same outcomes, the same principles and the same ambitions in life that hold us back from a real life because our society has been formed by the world around us, therefore we become limited in using our individuality and creativity towards the right things.

In the evolution of man, we developed legs mainly for the reason that we should walk the Earth just like what our nomadic forefathers did and not sit in front of our workstations or computers all day doing mundane things that we think are important. Unfortunately, the more we work and live in a modern society, the more we detach ourselves from the true essence of life. The more we cling to technology and social conformity, the more we become slaves to our unnecessary pursuits, thus we end up not living and fulfilling our lives with the internal realities. We all know there is something better out there and we know it isn't what the world has been offering us.

By embracing the New World Pilgrimage movement, we are encouraged to open our eyes and cast away our ideals to understand not only our environment but also our society as well as ourselves. Walking around this Earth will give us the optimal mind regarding everything that surrounds us.

The thing is that being a slave to modern society distracts and limits our true potential. We close ourselves from things and situations that do not conform our conditioned ideals. This is the reason why we tend to reject new ideas even if we know that new ideas are worth trying out. The thing is that we are scared to even admit that new ideas might work. If it does, it will mean the end of what we believe in.

The New World Pilgrimage helps us develop our true intellectual plasticity which is our minds' ability to accept and adapt to the new things that come into our lives. Because we are encouraged to walk this planet, we learn things on our journey. Learning and eventually adapting to the simple changes and greater challenges that we encounter.

Walking our planet will move not only our senses but it also helps us change the way we view our society as well as other people. We learn that technology and living in a modern society will never lead us to peace but will only make us slaves to modern fear, survival, and the conflict that is a result. This is the reason why it is so important that we embrace the New World Pilgrimage movement that eliminates the unnecessary.

Education

In order to become more competent individuals, we are exposed to our educational system even before we learn to speak intelligently. Education is necessary in our society and it secures us our future. This is the reason why parents invest a lot of money to send their children to good schools. However, is today's education really necessary? The answer is yes and no.

Education is important because it teaches us valuable information that we need in order to become more functional individuals in society. However, given that most of us are exposed to the traditional educational system, we eventually kill our creativity and individuality towards the simple things.

The problem is that conventional education does not promote individualism among many students. This is very paradoxical because young minds need to realize their individuality in order to become more confident and competent. Unfortunately, this paradox breeds confusion thus children grow up with limited mindset and doing only the things that are expected from them.

Unfortunately, there are many things that you are deprived of if we continue to be educated only within the confines of the four corners of our current educational system. In fact, even adults suffer too much from being taught following the mandates of our educational system. In fact, it is the limitation of our educational system that makes us prone to stereotyping other ideas. And this limitation breeds misunderstanding which robs us from the genuine peace that we deserve.

Education in the NWP

So how does the New World Pilgrimage give us hope towards our future educational system?

The first education, which we will call primary education, begins within the way stations like all other education to achieve their citizenship. Children will start to be educated on the basics of life, about food, maritime, clothing, shelter, distribution of food, law enforcement, route maintenance and other important lifesaving skills while walking in the wild. Of course, all these items will be taught to the child in an age appropriate manner and staggered until the child reaches twelve years old. Further, in each subject, the children will also have hands-on knowledge and experience such as going on field trips, camping and even doing mock trials to assess their skills and application of learning.

When they reach twelve years old, all students will begin their secondary education. They will be training in three different fields of work—this is whether they become active in growing crops, farming, food distribution, food development, building of shelter, maritime, route maintenance and law enforcement. These areas of responsibility will be tasked to them according to their area of expertise as shown in their primary education.

They will be trained by their proctors who are in the intermediate level. For each of their areas of responsibility, there will be three levels, the starting level, intermediate and the master's level.

During the starting level, they will be taught the ropes—and most of this will be hard labor. It would take at least 5 years to complete this level.

Next comes the intermediate level where he or she becomes a manager. He or she will manage his or her pool of starting students, will set the time, date and schedule of tasks that must meet the demands of the way station along with the demands of the arriving people who would need food, clothing and shelter before their next journey. Further, alongside their students, they should also work with them in the field and not just within the confines of his or her office. This stage will last up to two years,

depending on the performance of the
individual.

The last stage, the master's level means that
you have graduated from the intermediate
level and is now ready to become a master of
the three subjects you have been working on
for years now. Now, it is time for you to pass
on to little boys and girls what you have
learned—you will become a teacher. You will
be allowed to teach one to two subjects of
your choice for two years. While teaching,
you will also be demanded to study two more
additional areas of expertise which you can
choose freely that you think will help arm you
while walking the world. Each year, you can
change these chosen fields to your liking
whether you pass each subject or not.

Once you have served the necessary two
years of being a master, you are now a full-

fledged citizen of the New World Pilgrimage and you will be given a badge of a kind with your name on it. This will serve as your ticket and ID to all the ports of the world and to any way station.

Education as an NWP Citizen

Since we are encouraged to walk this planet, we end up meeting and talking with other people thus we learn about their background and adapt to them. By learning the lives of other people, we pick up very important learning along the way. And since we understand completely where they are coming from, we develop mutual respect to everyone we meet along our journey.

Aside from learning from other people, we also learn new ideas about life itself. The thing is that there are so many things the classroom of our school cannot teach us and by going out, we explore new things and learn all about these ideas. You will be stunned and amazed on how many new things you will encounter if you start your journey following the New World Pilgrimage movement. And even if you are forty, fifty or sixty years old, you will still be able to learn new and valuable ideas by walking this planet.

Imagine how much time we have wasted in educating ourselves and our children under the traditional educational system. We spend more than half of our lives learning things that we really never get to apply in the real world. What the New World Pilgrimage does is that it changes the way we think about education. New World Pilgrimage really focuses on the basics. Walking this earth and experiencing lessons in real life is the best education that we need to focus on. I believe that while conventional education is necessary for us to learn about the basic things like counting and reading words, walking this planet will teach us how to live meaningfully.

Libraries

Libraries are all over the world and while it is the best place to get the necessary information that we need to arm ourselves against ignorance. Libraries are treasure troves for those who want to learn different kinds of information about the world. However, it is crucial yet ironic to take note that ignorance starts inside libraries. The thing is that there are still over thousands of books that need to be rewritten and perhaps discarded as unnecessary because they contain ideas that are no longer applicable towards the new world.

New World Pilgrimage creates a new mindset. Unfortunately, books that need to be rewritten are still continuously displayed in the library. There is really no problem regarding displaying such books but the problem is that when young minds pick up these books and start reading and taking all information literally, it can change their mindset thus they end up becoming more deluded.

To make the situation more problematic, books also contain incorrect information. In fact, there are many history books that are written all wrong and do not give justice to some important historical events. Believing in incorrect information limits our way of thinking so we end up believing on incorrect information for a long time. As a result, it makes it difficult for us to unlearn all of the wrong information that we have passively gained from reading books and this goes for the old world culture of today. A new history would naturally be written in view of the new nomadic world of pilgrimage.

There is nothing really wrong about visiting the library, in fact it's good, but if we only spend our time inside such facility and do not explore our environment and society, we end up having limited point of views. There is really nothing like getting hands-on experiences in order to become more knowledgeable and adaptable to real life.

You may have not realized it yet but the world is a big library where you can learn many new things that you can also share with other people. Walking this planet gives you the opportunity to see the real situation of your society and learn from it. Instead of passive learning which is what visiting the library gives you, going out to the world is one of the best types of active learning. The best thing about active learning is that you learn new things fast and you also learn important life lessons faster and you also retain new lessons longer than passive learning.

The New World Pilgrimage lets you explore the vast information present in the library of life thus you will not need to spend too much time inside a brick and mortar library in order to learn the necessary information that you need. By walking this planet, you will be able to gain information faster and you are not restricted to learning only one thing but also a lot while you are still on a journey.

The world is a very big library and the only way to be able to learn from it is to start your journey in the New World Pilgrimage. It will open your eyes to the truth. You will be surprised on the many things that you will learn in your journey compared to visiting your library. After all, we will learn fast not because of books but rather because of our experiences.

Libraries in NWP will basically be found in gateway locations. There is much re-writing to do especially when it comes to the history and purpose of knowledge. New knowledge that supports and enhances walking the planet will be focused on, written, and therefore desired. Travel is physical life and the world is a book that eliminates the unnecessary. You can judge science, but you can't judge nature. Live a natural life.

Religion

Religion will not ever be allowed to rule in the era of New World Pilgrimage, but rather a nomadic and non-religious tenet will be in place. One that will enhance "free will" of all people in relationship with the internal elements of each soul. To maintain and create internal space is the task of New World Pilgrimage .Walking mediates this process in more ways than one. The world will be in such a utopian state that it will be easier for people to find inner peace within themselves and among others. Compare this to the blind pursue of the unnecessary we have all experienced in today's tumultuous world.

Although religion is often about joy and love towards other people, the concept of spreading love and joy is sometimes limited among those who are members of a religious way of life—and people outside of some religions are not part of the 'receivers' of good tidings historically. If you read historical books, you will notice that most wars that occurred during the ancient times did occur because of power struggles and religious differences. Try as we may deny it for example, Judaism, Christianity and Islam have always disagreed with one another even if we share the same prophets and biblical stories. In the New World Of Pilgrimage conflict of this type will not be tolerated. Conflicts such as these will be squashed. If you have some theological insight and wish to share it with the world, you will be free to do so while walking from station to station with others so long as the other is ok with it. You can also talk at the public forums provided at each station. When it comes to religious intolerance just know that religious intolerance will not be tolerated. Fighting over beliefs will be quelled by law enforcement. Each sect should also detract people from violence within their own group because there is really nothing to gain or acquire by being "right" in this way within the new world. There is no land, gold, or possessions to be had for winning such an argument. Most will simply laugh at such pointless outburst regarding religious debate.

Don't get me wrong here but I believe that religion is most important. However, wouldn't it also be nice if people become united beyond religion? When this happens, we will be able to achieve peace in our society.

The New World Pilgrimage is not bounded by religion thus you can walk this planet together with people who are also believers of a different religions yet still remain in harmony in your nomadic journey. The best thing about the New World Pilgrimage is that it enables us to get to know each other thus people become more open and more understanding to other's thoughts and point of view.

When you walk this planet, you may become engrossed in conversation while getting to know other people who are also on the same journey around the planet just like you. This allows you to see people for who they are. Simply put, the New World Pilgrimage helps us to cast aside our religious stereotypes created by possessive and excessive non-religious elements that are found presently in today's society so that we can actually have real time to enjoy the company of other people while on our long walk across the planet.

Some people may believe that the New World Pilgrimage wants to abolish religion thus they feel threatened towards this movement. However, this movement does not intend to do that. Religion is one of the oldest institutions in the world thus it is part of who we are. Faith is a dimension of what type of beings we are. What this movement aims to do is to bring all religious leaders to the clear understanding that the New World Pilgrimage is all about creating an environment of simplicity and tolerance which can be of value towards their own religious beliefs and personal progress.

The New World Pilgrimage serves as the middle road between all human difficulties and if you choose to travel your path to self-discovery and realization, you will realize that religion is better if it is able to expand itself and its ideals.

The New World Pilgrimage is tolerant of all religious beliefs, frees you from unnecessary burdens, and frees us so we can get to experience a higher and more advanced way of life. NWP makes this available to all people. Together these tenets form a responsible kind of freedom. New World Pilgrimage makes this possible for all people.

Law

Law is a system of rules that a particular country or community recognizes as regulating the actions of its members and the law they adapt may thereby enforce penalties for not following the rules that protect national interest.

Society is held by laws and this is the reason why nations have any order. In fact, countries are defined according to the laws that its populace follows. This means that if two people are citizens of one country, then they have to follow the same set of rules. When you get a cluster of people following the same rules and way of life in a given region they form what is known as a nation. Being raised and conditioned in any country people form a kind of pride and become loyal to family, community, and nation. This allegiance becomes an obstacle towards greater freedom.

Some nations have more resources than others or maybe just more valuable resources than another country. When one country doesn't have enough and it's people are suffering or another nation is just plain aggressive economically or militarily people rally together and sing patriotic songs. This leads to the unnecessary and ultimately towards evil.

Although nationalism was generally good and practical for its time, we must recognize that it limits our freedom and way of thinking. Nationalism has been the reason why we make decisions that may be good for our fellow countrymen but bad for our neighboring countries. Wars worldwide are examples. Today, wars are occurring between countries in the Middle East. Both countries believe or hope that waging war will bring good to their own countries but what they do not always realize is that it wreaks havoc on both nations.

The thing is that the restricting freedom that governs any nation creates borders and wars thus it makes it difficult for us to really find peace not only with ourselves but also to the rest of the people in the world. Most experts believe that the solution to war is to make warring countries and factions compromise and reconcile with one another. However, reconciliation is difficult to achieve if nationalism exist. In fact there are very few treaties that have ever been kept. In fact I can't think of one treaty that hasn't been broken. New World Pilgrimage integrates all people into a borderless walking society of free people.

Warring countries may ceasefire and achieve some degree of reconciliation but it may be soon after that they will start fighting again because of their nationalistic interest. It is a depressing cycle that we need to deal with if we do not address this situation properly. So what is the ideal way to solve conflicts because of the presence of nations? The answer is to give the people the freedom to walk the planet. To walk and complete the great trails and routes of the earth. This is the great hope of the new world to come.

The New World Pilgrimage is a movement that encourages you to walk the planet and cast aside your prejudice and ideologies. The movement is anti-nationalism because it firmly believes that nationalism breeds the undesirable and brings evil to

any society, a nation starts to seek safety, and because of this they close their borders and limits our ability to transverse the planet.

If nations are dissolved, people will be free to walk the earth according to the seasons just like our nomadic ancestors did. We are no longer enslaved with the concept of nationalism and country so we are able to get the resources that we need wherever resources are needed. This also prevents us from competing with other nations and exploiting our planet as well as other people.

People are afraid that if laws are abolished with the New World Pilgrimage, the world might get chaotic and dysfunctional. This will only happen if we have the wrong intentions to begin with. The natural order of things will be dictated by the goal which encourages us to walk and migrate according to the season without malice towards our fellow man so even if laws and nationalism are both abolished, we can still live peacefully under this movement because we become accountable to the welfare of other people. Now wouldn't it be nice to live in a world where you are free to walk and express your ideas? The goal of the New World Pilgrimage movement basically restores our hope and faith in humanity.

~ o ~

Chapter 3: Science of The Great Delusion

"Walk away quietly in any direction and taste the freedom of the mountaineer."
- John Muir

The world is full of mirages and we don't need to suffer from this delusional disorder in order to escape the reality that almost all of us will work indefinitely into old age just to survive. The mirage allowing us to only seeing the things that we think we really want to see. Things that have been pushed on us thru commercialism. In fact, society is full of delusions which prevents us from accepting the reality. This is the reason why many people feel a lot of negativities because delusion breeds desperation, disappointment and unhappiness. There are many facets in our lives where we often delude ourselves but there are only three great delusions that we should be aware that is eating at us, how we see reality, and how we live our lives.

Delusion at Work

The mantra "we work because we need to survive" is no longer being followed. Today, many people think that they live in order to work thus giving rise to millions of people enslaved to work until their deaths. Our dedication to our work gives us a false sense of happiness as we end up buying things in order to compensate for the long hours that we spend away from our families. Because of this, family and relationships crumble and people are neglected just so they can secure themselves at work.

To escape from the bludgeons of work, many people believe that the only way out is to become rich or to be patient and wait for retirement. Unfortunately, only a few really ever become wealthy or have saved enough for their retirement thus these strategies that most men heavily rely on will make them end up feeling disappointed as they face the final years of their lives. Some adapt and even convince themselves with a "positive" mindset just to cope with this dilemma, making the best of a pointless existence. Wouldn't it be better to think positively about the potential of a greater freedom?

This is a scary thought for almost all people and even if most people know about this reality, they still push forward blindingly because their delusional optimism towards a lesser freedom tells them that everything will be okay in the future. Hey, if you have thirty more years before retirement then you must believe that a lot of things can happen right? For all we know, you might strike good fortune when you reach the age of forty. But thinking like this is very wrong because it does not help you get out of the great delusion of work.

So how does the New World Pilgrimage break the delusion of work? In this novel paradigm, you work not because of yourself but your efforts are majorly geared towards other people. If people adapt to this new idea, then we work in support of the new society and once we have done our obligations, we are free to walk the earth.

Being concerned about your future has no place in the New World Pilgrimage. Of course, you might have some misgivings and doubts about how you can get the basic necessities such as food, clothing and shelter. Under the New World Pilgrimage, other people will be the ones to supply them for you once you reach the prime of your life just as you had supplied these things to others during your working time in the support system.

The New World Pilgrimage lets you work for the benefits of other so that you can also benefit from other people as you get older. This new exchange system is unlike any other because it allows you to enjoy your job supplying basic needs within the support system for a relatively short span of time. Moreover, you also become less enslaved towards work thus you will have more time to enjoy the beauty of life and all things that go with it.

The thing is that our work is one of the things that holds us back from doing the things that we love. Traveling and securing our future is the end game even in our times. With the New World Pilgrimage, we will be able to just that, travel and have a future where we can make the most out of our lives.

Delusion of Convenience and Comfort

In today's society, most of us want comfort and convenience. Unfortunately, seeking comfort and convenience often leads us to throw our logic and common sense out of the window just so we can pursue the things that will make us feel good.

We cannot escape the fact that comfort and convenience rule us in many ways that we can imagine. The urbanization of many countries as well as the increase in our credit card debts are clear indications that we seek things that will give us comfort and convenience. In fact, we huddle in places where we can be close to all the things that will make our lives easy and we also borrow money or max out our credit cards in order to feel comfortable.

Unfortunately, our innate obsession for comfort and convenience is killing us, as well as robbing us from the best things that life has to offer. For one, we throw away our society and it also destroys relationship. For example, the reason why divorce rate is very high is because many couples no longer feel convenient in their relationship as husbands and wives. Our quest of comfort and convenience now gives us the option to always take the easy way out. Wouldn't it be nice to know that people want to really be with you? For the simple reason that they enjoy your company and want to be around you? Instead of wondering if they really like you or only like you for the comforts you provide them.

To make matters worse, we pass on our affinity for comfort and convenience to our offspring as though these traits are hereditary. This is the reason why kids today grow up to be self-entitled, lazy, less adaptable and less tolerant to the changes that come their way. In fact, most kids today would cringe to small problems like breaking a nail and think that it is already the end of the world. Compare that to our forefathers who have lived simply and strive hard to face each problem that they encounter head on.

Because of our quest to seek comfort and convenience, we shun away from self-discipline and accountability. Unfortunately, these are the two things that we need in order to live our lives to the fullest.

With the New World Pilgrimage, it breaks our habit of always seeking out comfort and convenience so that we can enjoy the finer and truer things in our lives. Because this idea encourages us to walk this earth in a simple manner, we are able to cast off things that bring us false comfort and convenience.

Moreover, we also open our eyes and realize that the most important things in our lives are those that money cannot buy.

The New World Pilgrimage works in a support system thus we end up seeking comfort and convenience from people within the system. As we walk this earth under New World Pilgrimage, we tend to find comfort on things that truly matter and not on things that society tells us that matters.

Comfort and convenience provide false hopes to individuals and if you are a slave of it, you will never know what duty, service, fortitude and sacrifice are. With the New World Pilgrimage, it simply changes the way you think about comfort and convenience. In today's society we enslave people for a lifetime to bring all the "extras" of today's world of outdated thinking. In the New

World Pilgrimage you will find new comforts and conveniences based on the basics of food, shelter, and clothing.

Delusion of Surplus

It is part of human nature to desire many things. In fact, we are the most dissatisfied organisms to have ever walked this planet. This is the reason why the world is full of extras and surplus. Having a lot of extras and surplus gives us a false sense of hope and security. I believe that people are deluded to thinking that surplus provides cushion and security in times when supply is low. This is also the reason why many people believe that having too much of things is linked to affluence.

The delusion of surplus is very evident in today's society. It is natural for us to own too much of one thing. For instance, we own and use different types of mobile phones to call our families, work peers, friends and other acquaintances. We also use different kinds of credit cards to make different types of purchases. Our reason for this is that, by identifying with the concept of surplus, we can easily manage our lives simply.

The problem with extras and surpluses is that it is not only people who suffer but also our planet. Among people, the most common effect of embracing surpluses is that we tend to develop the habit of hoarding. We also become more obsessed with our material things and we also end up competing with other people. We become impersonal towards how we deal with other people.

On the other hand, surplus and extras can also wreak havoc to the planet. Remember that we only have one planet and that the resources of our planet are not infinite. With our obsession for surplus, we also end up competing with space—storage. The packaging alone of all these individual items is enough to choke the planet. It has been our quest to amass wealth and material things that led us to encroach unexplored landscapes to build cities, roads and even theme parks. We not only displace animals but also other people in this process.

Wouldn't it be nice to eliminate these things? The elimination of material things like money is perhaps one of the most ideal solutions on how to solve such problem. Elimination of surplus results to many things. One of the benefits is that we tend to become more contented with what we have. Moreover, it also encourages us to work in achieving the things that we need. Lastly, because extras are eliminated, we give our planet a time to heal itself as we no longer compete for it for space.

So how do we break the delusion of extras? The New World Pilgrimage is one of the concepts that can help up break this delusion. The New World Pilgrimage instills novel ideas on how we can live in this planet simply. The world does not need us to leave a lot of things behind and that is what we are certainly doing when we become slaves to extras and surpluses. So walk the New World Pilgrimage now so that we can drop all the extra things that hamper us from growing into meaningful individuals.

~ o ~

Chapter 4: The Natural Path

"For my part, I travel not to go anywhere, but to go. I travel for travel's sake. The great affair is to move."
– Robert Louis Stevenson

The New World Pilgrimage is a new movement that allows people from all over the world to do drastic changes in their lives as well as radiate the goodness to society. It is a movement unlike any other because it teaches people to start a lifestyle revolution so that we can explore limitless opportunities. In this movement, you are encouraged to drop all of your baggage and enjoy the splendor that nature and humanity has to offer. In this chapter, we will talk about how the New World Pilgrimage can benefit people in terms of how they uphold their lifestyle as well as exchange ideas with society.

The Natural

There are many reasons why people embark on a journey and join the New World Pilgrimage movement. Some people want to walk for peace while some walk to find their inner spirituality and enlightenment. Whatever reasons you have for undergoing an arduous journey, you walk and commune with nature.

This movement encourages you to walk for long distances and whether you walk all by yourself or accompanied by other people, you can learn a lot of things from walking on natural environments. It does not matter if you walk in the desert or you pass by the urban jungle, walking this planet helps you learn important life lessons that you will learn from nature itself.

One of the things that we get benefit out of walking our planet is that we put down our roots. This means that we are grounding ourselves for the benefit of our personal growth. If we are grounded, it gives us a sense of freedom to grow in any way that we want and still share compassion to other people.

Another thing that we learn from nature is that we tend to become more flexible. Just like plants, we are able to learn how to be in the now with the changes thus allowing us to become more welcoming to new things. If you start your journey, you end up being able to change and accommodate the things that life throws your way—without getting stressed about it.

Not only do we get enough sunshine if we start our journey following this movement but we also continue to grow despite adversities. You might be parched and feel dispirited while you are undergoing a long pilgrimage but you will learn important lessons that will help you grow as a better individual.

Self-discovery is one of the things that you can also benefit from embarking on the New World Pilgrimage. It is advantageous to you especially if you are a person who has yet to find your self-worth. In this life, we seek our real reasons and purposes for living. Whether you acknowledge it or not, it is part of our human psyche to seek our purpose of living and this is the reason why we tend to seek our reasons in all the wrong places.

By walking this earth and embracing a lifestyle revolution, you will be able to get the realization that you are a unique person. By being one with nature, you realize that everything in life has a purpose even if it is just a weed. The thing is that you do not need to pay other people to tell you that you are a unique person. Walking this earth will help you realize that.

You owe it to yourself to take the natural path for self-discovery as well as self-realization. This is the only way to achieve all of the important things in life. It may take you a long journey towards self-discovery but you will learn a lot of things about yourself, others, your environment and everything else if you follow the New World Pilgrimage movement.

The New Exchange

The New World Pilgrimage movement is a borderless system that encourages people to walk the earth in order to abolish nationalism and cultural isolation. By abolishing the boundary, it also helps us expand what we know about the concept of freedom.

This non-violent revolution will crumble all nations in the world but this should not scare you from embracing the movement. The thing is that society is bounded by limitations— limitations in the form of political regime and ideologies born out of culture. Because of these limitations, we end up not being able to see the real things that are going on around us. Moreover, they also rob us the joy of communing with our family, friends as well as nature.

It is interesting to take note that joining this movement and embarking on a nomadic pilgrim can also teach us how we perceive life as well as how we interact with people. Since the New World Program is all about walking the planet with only the clothes on your back, you get to work your way to provide the things that you need.

The New World Program teaches you to walk in the planet and, at the same time, work for the benefit of other people. Once you are done providing for other people, you can continue your journey and they will be the one to provide you for your needs like shelter, clothing and food. The thing is that the New World Program movement makes you accountable for other people and you get the benefits through the pay-it-forward system.

This novel idea for exchanging with other people is something that has never been done and it is exciting to take note that the only thing that we need to do to "pay" for or get what we need is to be accountable to other people's needs. Our accountability to other people is a selfless way of working to provide our needs and what the New World Pilgrimage does is that it allows us to inspire other people and leave big impacts in their lives so that, one day, they will also follow this movement out of their own volition. Aside from the new concept of exchange of goods the New World Pilgrimage, this movement also promotes the exchange of limitless ideas. Since this nomadic pilgrimage helps people unlearn their ideologies and learn new ones, a new exchange of ideas is also born out of the New World Pilgrimage movement.

By exchanging new ideas, we are able to open new doors for the world so that we will be able to create a utopian environment for our children in the future. Some people believe that it is impossible to do this but if we can make a big impact in the world with this movement, then anything is possible. The novel way of exchanging ideas will only be achieved if we embrace the New World Pilgrimage and start walking this planet. After all, we have two feet and we have to use it.

~ o ~

Chapter 5: Walking

"Travel, in the younger sort, is a part of education; in the elder, a part of experience."
— Francis Bacon

The idea about the New World Pilgrimage is to start your journey by walking this planet. You may walk all by yourself or with a group of people. However you do it, you have to remember to keep up with your journey in order to get to your destination. There have been many people who have already tried to walk on a pilgrimage and they have different reasons why they do it. If you want to start your own personal journey, then it is important that you need to know about the pilgrimage way of life.

Being on a pilgrimage can be tough but very rewarding. Those who have done it for the first time encounter some problems, initially, but as soon as they were able to get on their pace, they were able to enjoy their journey.

Walking

Walking is undoubtedly what you need to do if you want to start your journey. In most cases, most people who are in pilgrimage need to walk long distances under different types of weather conditions. And as someone who is dedicated in finishing the journey, it is important that you tread under different weather conditions no matter how convenient or hard they may be.

However, it is important that all people will have a goal to walk the planet at least once in their lives. Walking with a purpose does not only give a lot of benefits to the physical body but it also gives you the sense of appreciation of what nature can give you. Remember that staying in one place only creates stagnation so it is important that you walk this planet and enjoy the beauty and lessons that it can give you.

For people who start the journey for the very first time can be very difficult. What makes it difficult is that you have to adapt to the new changes as soon as you start your journey. Everything will definitely be different—new people, new sceneries and new environment —thus it is important that you know how to adjust to your life while in your journey.

Another thing that makes the journey difficult in the beginning is carrying a backpack all the time. Your backpack contains everything that you need in order to survive while you are on a pilgrimage. Aside from the weight of your backpack, you also need to bring a limited number of things thus you end up casting aside a lot of things that usually bring you comfort. Adjusting to life on a journey can be challenging especially if you are someone who cannot live without your gadgets—assuming that NWP can commence in our lifetime.

When preparing for your journey, it is important that you practice first by walking a few distances within your community so that you will be able to get used to it once you start your journey. Another thing that you need to prepare before you start your journey is to have a pair of good walking shoes that fits you perfectly. So, it is always best to check your shoes while resting on way stations and procure one if needed rather than risk being shoeless halfway through your journey.

Another obstacle that you need to take note of when walking on a pilgrimage is to make sure that you protect yourself against the elements of weather. Wearing comfortable clothes is very important during hot weather. On the other hand, you should also have sturdy and warm clothing to protect you from the cold. Even though people will migrate to warmer climates in the winter it can still get cold at night in Summer and higher elevations.

Only bring what is necessary so that you can save space in your backpack. The necessary things that your bag should include clothing to fend the cold or the hot sun, first aid kit, water canteen, knife, and maybe a diary to document your journey if needed—this is if you want to be prepared. However, Pilgrims can also opt not to carry too much stuff when walking. The way stations (way zones) are not too far apart. Water fountains are one mile apart; the trails are shaded by fruit and nut trees as much as possible. The trails will be continually re-forested with all things edible by the support system.

Walking and starting a journey is the most worthwhile thing that you can do in your life. To avoid any obstacles while you are on the road, you should prepare yourself not only spiritually but also physically and mentally.

Mass Migration

In a general sense, migration is defined as the movement of people over a significant distance. However, in modern times, migration is often referred to the movement of migrants from one country to the other. Moreover, migration today seemed to be influenced heavily by economic or political reasons.

However, this is not the case for the New World Pilgrimage. This movement encourages people to walk the planet for self-discovery. It is challenging but it has been done by some groups and organizations. For instance, the Velitokeretsky Procession of the Cross in Russia attracts more than 40,000 pilgrims to converge and go on a 5-day pilgrimage following and carrying the icon of the wonder-worker, St. Nicolay. All kinds of people come and join the pilgrimage whether they are healthy or sick, rich or poor, old or young—it doesn't matter. To one guy, what matters is that during the pilgrimage, "you forget about problems and money which take the center stage in everyday life—you think above all these problems and that's what the pilgrims find important; because if you don't do this from time to time, you fade away inside and die as a person and just become some kind of walking dead."

There are things that need to be addressed before starting the mass migration which is the ultimate aim of the New World Pilgrimage movement. One of the things that need to be considered include the "gateways" where people can converge to start the migration, routes, trails as well as access to resources.

The gateway, as the name implies serve as the venue where thousands of people can meet up to start a migration. It has yet to be established all over the world. Gateways are supposed to be large crossroad areas that are connected to a network of migration trails, routes and way stations. Moreover, it should also serve as stop-over points where people can pass through to document their accomplishments so that they become full citizens of the world instead of being only restricted to one country. Gateways are around 500 to 1,000 miles away from each other. These places will be bigger hubs of technology and science where computers are maintained for the purpose of verifying pilgrim passages. Gateways will also be places where voting is done.

In order to start the movement, each continent should have a number of key gateways where people can document their journey. Since it will serve as a strategic point, gateways should also house the world's major libraries so that people will have access to the necessary information that they need.

Another thing that needs to be addressed in mass migration is the routes and trails. People should be given options on which routes that they should take. Today, there are only a few routes and trails that are established and most of these routes are not connected. However, when the New World Pilgrimage will be embraced different pilgrimage routes from all over the world will be connected so it will be easier for pilgrims to converge at the end of the trail.

Mass migration influenced by the New World Pilgrimage has yet to happen but the idea where people can do mass migration within a network of trails for self-discovery is likely possible if we tend to push this movement towards other people. If they begin to understand.

Routes and Trails

Getting on a self-journey or pilgrimage requires you to take on routes and trails. However, those who want to partake in the New World Pilgrimage movement may find it difficult to find trails near them. Moreover, to make matters more difficult, most of the routes and trails scattered all over the world are not connected to one another. Some people follow the trails while some start a trail of their own. If it is your first time to walk the planet, it is important that you know the many trails where you can start your pilgrimage. The main routes around the planet will be maintained by the workforce and can be trans-versed globally by large groups of people.

Way Stations and Gateways

In this section, I will give more focus on the way stations which are very important aspects of the New World Pilgrimage movement. In general, way stations are comfort zones that are similar to base camps when climbing a mountain. The way zones provide mass produced fresh food to accommodate different kinds of diets for guest. They will also have rooms where people can stay for the night. However, if there is an overflow of guests, outdoor tents will also be provided.

Being true to its name, way zone also has entertainment such as music provided by the travelers as well as those working in the support system. Everyone gets a chance to interact with other people that way. Moreover, there will also be forums for people to express their views including their religious and artistic views.

The support network will be manned by seasoned travelers who have circumnavigated the planet when they were younger. There will be election of elders to establish harmony within the support system so that the basic needs will be provided to the travelers without any problems.

It is interesting to take note that way stations will not look like hotels but they will have interesting architecture with interesting art such as sculptures, monuments, paintings and murals done by those that have the ability, the travelers in some cases, and generally

those who work in the support system.
Everything is provided for in way stations but
unlike hotels, the services come with a
personal touch. Way stations serve as tiny
communities at the end of the trail providing
support not only to travelers but also to
those who work in the support system.

Gateways on the other hand, are a much
bigger way stations; it is like a capital city.
Gateways are designated places of voting and
verification—wherein you and other people
can verify your walking progress.
Documenting continents traveled, they would
be places where voting would take place,
hubs for technology, and libraries. Gateways
would maintain highly functional computers
and global networks for data and verification
of pilgrim passages. If there is any breakdown
in this system a more simple back-up process
will also be in place.

Natural Wonders

Traversing the planet with only a backpack and a walking stick is what the New World Pilgrimage movement is all about. Those who wish to start their own journey need to follow a trail which is usually found in off-beaten locations. For this reason, pilgrims will be able to commune with nature.

Pilgrims do not only traverse cities and towns during their journey, but also the remnants of ancient sites and the more recently abandoned civilization of today. Perhaps the most important part of the walk is passing along natural wonders. Most of the trails are near great natural wonders like canyons, waterfalls and mountain peaks around the world. There will be trails along the sea, the lake as well as rivers thus you not only enjoy the splendor of nature but you will also be able to learn important life lessons from nature.

Wouldn't it be nice to take on a journey and traverse the Grand Canyons or the hot springs of Pamukkale in Turkey before you proceed to the River Jordan in Israel? Or what about pass the ancient ruins in Greece before you go straight ahead to the edge of the Sahara desert? Or how does walking the entire length of Southeast Asia and enjoy the beauty of the lush jungles in Borneo before proceeding to the rice paddies of Thailand appeal to you? With the New World Pilgrimage, visiting these natural wonders is very possible. Nobody will stop you from visiting the places that you thought impossible to reach.

What most people might have is the apprehension of taking routes that are off the beaten path because they fear that they will not be able to sustain themselves during the long journey. But when the New World Pilgrim support network expands, even remote areas will have way stations where pilgrims can recharge themselves even if the trails that they have taken on are desolate.

While on your pilgrimage, you will also learn how to be accountable towards retaining the beauty of the natural wonders that you pass so that other travelers will also be able to witness the grandeur of nature in the future. As a result, you become a member of the support network that promotes your accountability towards other people as well as to the environment while you are in a journey.

With the New World Pilgrimage, you embark a journey to self-discovery and, at the same time, enjoy the best field trips that you will ever have in your life. When you go on an extended journey and see the beautiful sceneries around you, you will realize how small and insignificant you are compared to the marvelous natural wonders that surround you and despite your size, you have the power and initiative to affect nature based on decisions that you make.

The New World Pilgrimage movement simply teaches you to become more in one with nature without having to worry about surviving your very long journey. Moreover, you will be able to make only the best choices for your journey as well as for the environment.

Food or Agriculture

Going on a journey to self-discovery is not an easy task. There are many concerns that you need to address and one of them is where to get your food. Today, people who plan to go long distance walking often carry their own food because it is difficult to find supplies especially if you are in the middle of a rural trail.

Food supplies can be a problem for most travelers but with the New World Pilgrimage movement, you can go on your personal journey without the need to worry about where you will get your next meal. How is it possible?

The New World Pilgrimage movement is made up of a network system where all pilgrims help each other on their journey. There will be way stations that will be scattered all over the network of trails all over the world where travelers can get their food and replenish their stocks. The way stations may be five or ten miles apart depending on the type of terrain that the pilgrims need to walk on so they can be assured that at the end of their trip, they will be able to find food to recharge their energies.

On the other hand, the support network is also responsible in planting fruit trees and vegetation along the trail which the pilgrims can utilize as emergency rations. Fruit trees, shrubs and berries will be planted along the way and will be cared for by other pilgrims so that they can get fruits whenever they go hungry. The trees that will be planted will be local trees that have adapted to the local weather where the trails are located.

This means that trails in Southeast Asia will be planted with local varieties of fruits like mangoes, jackfruit and other tropical fruits

while those in the temperate regions will be planted with fruit trees that can adapt to their climate. The best thing about getting local vegetation along the trail is that they are free. You only need to pay for the food by being accountable to other people.

The New World Pilgrimage encourages many people from different religions to walk the planet and the best thing about this movement is that the way stations provide food for different religions. They also prepare food for small or large groups so there is really nothing to worry about food preferences among different people.

Another problem related to food is the waste. The New World Pilgrimage discourages the use of artificial packaging so the trail will be kept clean. Regarding food scraps, you can return it to the earth so that it will rot and turn into rich fertilizer for other plants. Moreover, the movement of the food will also be revolutionized as there will be a rail network which is used to transfer food from one station to the other for pilgrims convenience.

And since the New World Pilgrimage movement encourages people to become stewards of the environment, pilgrims are also encouraged to leave behind something like a seed so that it will grow into a tree and other pilgrims can also benefit from it in the future.

The food found along the trail will be free for everyone to use. However, it is important to know that you should only get food that you can consume. Do not get too much food that you throw the excess out. Think about the welfare of your fellow pilgrims. Moreover, getting too much food simply breeds greed and the movement does not have any room for such negativities or it will crumble. Besides you wouldn't be able to carry large quantities of food long distance, so it really isn't an issue.

The New World Pilgrimage is all about looking out for the environment as well as for other people so that we can get the things that we need from the system like food without having to worry about paying for them. This is a perfect system that we should emulate soon.

Wildlife

Aside from passing by natural wonders along the trail, pilgrims will also encounter wildlife especially along rural trails or routes. Wildlife encounter is one of the most wonderful experiences that you will ever have. In fact, such encounter will make you realize that life is a gift and that we share this planet with other organisms as well. It simply reminds us that we are not alone and that as the organism who is blessed with so much intellectual capacity, we should serve as stewards of all living things.

Unfortunately, this is not the case among many people who decide to walk long distances as they also feel threatened whenever they see animals along their trail such as bears, wild cats and even snakes. While it is true that the main instinct of animals is to attack people in the wild, this will not happen unless you have encroached their territory or you have given them any signs that you are a threat to their safety.

So what do you do if you find a bear or snake along the way. If you can spot it immediately from afar, stop whatever you are doing and slowly back away until the animal leaves the trail. You can only walk the trail unless the animal is a safe distance away from the trail. On the other hand, hunting packs like wolves or lions can also be a problem because they attack in offense and not on defense.

Should hunting animals scare you off to postpone segments of your journey? No.

Although you have to walk in the rural trail most of the time, the New World Pilgrimage movement will only establish trails that are safe for everyone. This means that you will not walk along trails where dangerous animals are known to prowl in the area. If such trail does exist, you will be given a warning in the way station on what kind of wildlife you will expect in a trail and how you can protect yourself if the animals are dangerous.

Moreover, since there will be many people who will be walking the planet, the trails will have heavy foot traffic thus you can get support from other pilgrims whenever you encounter some wildlife problems. But such things rarely happen unless you show some signs of aggression towards the animal. So when you walk this planet, be sure to walk lightly so as not to attract the attention of bigger animals.

Moreover, it is also crucial that you avoid walking at night because this is the time when bigger animals are most active. This is the reason why way stations will be established so that you can stay safe during the evening and rest so that you may continue your journey at daybreak.

Encountering wildlife and observing their activities is the most humbling experience that you will ever have if you embark on a long journey. This will make you appreciate how good nature is and how important your role is in protecting them. Through NWP, The planet will again be filled with wildlife on land & in the sea.

Water

Water is life and it is important that you replenish your supply of clean water when you start your long journey. Perhaps one of the most important hiking tools that you need to bring is a big canteen which you can use to fill with water. Moreover, the type of terrain also influences your water intake. If you are taking on a flat terrain, you won't need to exert too much energy so your water requirement will not be too much. However, if you tread on rugged terrains, then you will need to drink water all the time to hydrate yourself. However, water containers can only hold enough water so what do you do when you run out of water?

The best thing about the New World Pilgrimage movement is that it relies so much on the support network from other pilgrims so you do not need to worry about where and how to get clean water. You will be surprised that the system will provide your needs even if you are in the middle of the mountain trail. You will also be directed to a clean well or a mountain spring where you can get your water supply on more remote trails is you choose to use them. In most cases, springs are located along the trail so you do not need to go far.

You do not need to deviate from your trail to look for a nearby river or stream. If you do that, you will only waste a lot of time. All networks of trails established by the movement will have sources of water nearby which you share with the local support people. Every trail has designated drinking stations where you can get your much-needed clean water.

The trails also have directions on where you can get water to replenish your supply so all you need to do is to follow the signs so that you can get your water.

Aside from getting water along the trail, you can also replenish your water supply from the many way stations. The way stations will supply you with clean water aside from food and shelter. Moreover, they also have plumbing where you can get water so that you can use the toilet as well as take a bath. Since water stations are strategically placed all over the network of trails, you do not need to worry about carrying a big jug to contain your water. You can travel light and get your water whenever you need it.

The idea of providing water along the trail is a great idea because it helps pilgrims to focus on more important parts of their journey.

Pilgrims do not need to spend most of their energy on worrying about where to find their basic needs including water so you can just focus your energy on your journey and your purpose of undergoing such journey.

The New World Pilgrimage movement is a journey unlike any other as it has the best support system so that pilgrims can focus on their journey and not on where to look for their basic necessities. This will make the journey more interesting and meaningful.

~ o ~

Chapter 6: Walking Society

"The World is a book, and those who do not travel read only a page."
– Saint Augustine

Now that you have an idea of what walking means and how it would affect mass migrations, routes and trails, natural wonders, food and agriculture, wildlife and water we will now focus our attention on the walking society.

People have always lived in groups—which makes it easier for us to lead our lives. Living in a society entails specializations in terms of work and division of labor so that we can be free to pursue other goals. Plus the fact that, people are social animals and as such have always lived in groups—whether in a family, close knit community or society as a whole.

But, just like in any society, there are rules and so with the New World Pilgrimage. However, the New World Pilgrimage rules are not stifling like rules, regulations, state law's, ordinances and whatnots that we currently have. As I have mentioned earlier, NWP is an open-source—a work in progress where people can add their ideas to make it better and more effective in leading a nomadic life.

Way Stations

The first thing that you need to know and understand in the walking society is way stations. Way stations are like rest stops or places where people can get life's necessities in between their nomadic journey around the planet.

I envision way stations to be five to ten miles away from each other, depending on the terrain and space. Gateways on the other hand will be 500 to 1000 miles away from each other.

It can be a big place or a small community, but either way each way station is self-sufficient. It has its own primary school, secondary school and the sources to provide for the community and for each of the pilgrims that passes by the way station. In short, a way station is sufficient by itself however it does not have the computers that gateways have to verify a pilgrim's progress. Further, no voting ever takes place within a way station. Basic medicines might be produced within the way zones, mostly natural remedies—perhaps pain medicines and antibiotics.

Where Citizens of NWP can get Provisions

At way stations, people can get replenishment for their food, clothing, shelter, water, medicines and whatever else they would need—for free. If they want to stay on for a while, they are free to stay before continuing on to their journey and as long as there is space for arriving pilgrims. In this case a tent may be provided or you may have to move on to the next station. Keeping the flow is important.

If journeying citizens decide to stay for a while in a certain way station to start a family that is also possible. But, the parents or at least one parent would need to do at least two areas of responsibility—preferably the ones that they have mastered while in secondary school.

Others have proposed that parents can also leave their kids within a way station starting at a certain age and just come back once they have traveled the world on foot which basically takes 5 years. This decision is not a to be taken lightly that's why those who are planning to start a family should take matters seriously and bring up their family as befits their plans.

Hub for Society

Way stations will be a society where people can live in semi-permanently to house or educate their children, to rest from the constant walking or simply just to replenish their stuff before heading to a new direction. The people who live here are tasked to take care of the constant influx of people, to serve and meet their needs until such time that they graduate and become full-fledged citizen of the new world.

People with Disabilities

People with disabilities, most often than not, will live their life in one way station. But, they are still free to walk the world given that they have competent companions. People with disabilities will also need to help around the way station and will be treated no differently than other people with no disabilities, provided that they are of sound mind and judgment.

However, if people with disabilities decide not to walk the world, they will always have a special place within the way station. Further, they can go on a walk to fulfill their spiritual needs. Some who have physical walking limitations may be able to take on larger supervisory roles as needed according to their abilities.

Relationships

Before we delve further into relationships, it is important to let you know that: Families are important, but the goal is priority and family secondary to the goal. Families happen even when couples are not really capable of bringing up children, so family cannot dictate the direction of society. Instead the goal (walking the planet) provides the structure and role of people in society. Families naturally populate the earth, but are not to direct society nor the lifetime goal of walking the earth. The life goal of pilgrimage keeps the world fluid, like a river, providing the greater motivation and freedom for people. The goal maintains a natural ratio of production and freedom.

Relationships in the New World Pilgrimage are bigger and wider. People should care for one another just as if they were brothers and sisters—because if we promote strong family ties within blood relations, problems and obstacles can easily arise from this situation. Having strong family ties per se is not the problem, the problem stems from too much love of the family and having no love for your neighbors. Your love for your family should be equal to your love of your neighbors. This way, it is ensured that everybody will take care of each other.

Just take for example, if people loved their family so much and there was some food shortage, do you know up to what lengths that person would go to just to protect his or her family at the detriment of other people or to society as a whole? Further, a person with too much love of family and no love of his brethren can become clannish and would lead to discontent, envy and even war. This would also lead to favoritism in the school, work or wherever you may be. Therefore, treat others as you would treat yourself or your beloved family.

Starting a Family

Starting a family is a very important decision. As parents, you should be open to the possibility that you will leave your child in the way station as you walk around the world. It may be five years before you would see each other again. But, rest assured, you would know that your child will be in good hands because as we have mentioned earlier, citizens of NWP loves one another just as much as they love their family.

You can also stay in the way station to rear your child, to rear your family, until such time that you deem it's appropriate to leave your child or children in the hands of other caretakers and pursue your pilgrimage together with your wife or husband.

However, if parents do decide to leave their child behind in the way station, they can only do so once the kid is at least eight years old and ready to start his or her primary schooling. This way, the children can be left in the boarding school along with other kids of their age. This is another decision to consider heavily, but as conditioning from the old world dissolves, a new sense of family will form, where this way of life will become the norm. If you look at today world parents' divorce and leave children behind in many cases, so this is not so uncommon even in our current times.

Marriage or partnership is to be taken seriously as to live in a station support area is very basic with no frills, just a small room for sleeping, access to clean water, and food, and education for children.

Different cultures in the past have carried infants on their backs while working, so the option of walking is also quite possible for families, but eventually children need to remain in one place for education in order to become citizens.

Daily Life

You might be thinking what would daily life be like in the New World Pilgrimage movement? Basically, you will have three different lifestyles, which will be discussed in detail below:

Primary School

At this stage, the 8-year old child will begin their first year in school. They will be taught the basics of math, science, English, activities of daily life and the areas of responsibilities in NWP. This will help them hone skills that they would need to serve within the NWP community and to help them get ready for their pilgrimage. They will be equipped with the survival skills needed.

So a typical day would be at 9 a.m. classes would start and end by 11:30 a.m. for the lunch break. They would be back in their classrooms by 1 PM, followed by a short 30-minute break by 3 PM and classes would end at 5 PM. The children would return to their respective homes or to their boarding house and help with the chores like food preparation or tidying up the place.

Secondary School

Since in secondary school there are 3 stages, so each will be discussed differently.

Beginners – during the first stage of secondary school from 12 to 17 years of age, typically, they will spend most of the day working in the field depending on which area of responsibility they have been assigned to.

Their day would start at 7 am and end by 5 pm with a two hour break divided into 3 breaks. At the end of the day, they are to return to their homes or boarding school and are free to do as they please.

Intermediate – Basically, the students in this level have the same hours as the stage one, but half of the time is spent on management duties and the other half of the time is spent in training and helping out in the field work alongside the students assigned to them. The intermediate students who are in their second year are tasked to help the first year intermediate students in learning the ropes of their management duties and will also be considered their head.

Masters – Once you are a Master, you are required to teach students in school. You will be devoting half of your day in teaching students and the other half of the day learning a new area of responsibility. After 5 pm, the masters are free to do as they please.

Citizens of NWP

Most of the time, citizens of NWP would be walking the Earth. They will also have the time to sit down, relax and contemplate their spiritual journey. If they are travelling with other people, they can have some entertainment around a campfire with songs and stories of their adventures. They will also have to spend time hunting or gathering food, refilling their canteen of water from water sources.

Health

As for the health of NWP followers, majority of them are healthy because of their active lifestyle. There will be no hospitals to treat the sick, what people can turn on to is to take good care of themselves in order to prevent sickness. They can also make use of herbal medicines that they can use while on the move, but basically there will be no pharmaceuticals to give them pills for any ailment. People will live and die in a natural way and from natural causes without being propped up by artificial means. There will be no surgeries and no surgeons. Citizens of NWP have to face this fact and accept this liberating way of life.

Each way station will have infirmaries for the sick were they will be cared for with in basic care. There will be knowledgeable people to help with your basic healthcare needs. Here at the most you will find pain medicine and simple antibiotics. A place where bones can be reset to a degree, and a place to quarantine viruses.

With the New World taking the best knowledge in personal hygiene, plumbing, sanitation, fresh natural food sources, water, clean air, healthy work, great walks, simple joys, entertainment, laughter, and ultimate relaxation. The nomadic world of health will be brighter than has ever been in human history. People will live healthy quality lives.

Nature is good. You cannot judge nature, but we can judge science. To avoid the unnatural in the medical sciences liberates the world.

"Walking is man's best medicine" -
Hippocrates Greek physician (460 BC - 377 BC)

Chapter 7: Rough Spots

"A good traveler has no fixed plans, and is not intent on arriving."
– Lao Tzu

Every man should partake in a chance to walk around the earth once in his lifetime. Walking the planet has a lot of benefits as it widens your horizon, gives you time to evaluate your ideologies and makes you more aware of the things that are happening around you. However, embarking on a long journey can be an arduous task and if you are one of the many people who have yet to circumnavigate the planet, then here are the rough spots that you need to be aware of.

Industry

Because of the liberating nature of New World Pilgrimage the aim of the new nomadic society is to free up time for pilgrimage, seeing the world, and traveling in the most responsible and liberating way possible which is on foot. In the New World Pilgrimage all industry is for the purpose of supplying the way stations with food, shelter, and clothing. There will be no other purpose for industry as there is no money and personal accumulation of wealth. You would not be able to just run off into the woods and start building things on your own. In this respect the society functions collectively in order to allow more individual time and freedom to travel on foot.

Resources

Embarking on a journey following the principles of the New World Pilgrimage is not your usual camping trip. In this journey, you are encouraged to travel light and take only the things that really matter to you such as a few items of foods and water to hydrate you on the long journey.

The New World Pilgrimage movement does not intend you to go hungry as each trail has way stations where you can get your food, water and shelter. It's just that once you start traveling during the day, you have to make do with what you have until you reach the next station.

The limited resources while traveling is a curse among undisciplined people who travel for leisure but it will teach you a lot of things like how to ration the few items you bring with you. Although you cannot get regular meals until you reach the way station, the trails are lined with edible fruits and plants that you can eat as alternative sources of energy so you will not really go totally hungry. In fact, this journey will also teach your stomach to behave.

There will also be smaller stands of fruit, nuts, and berries along between stations depending on the amount of laborers in a region. When available these small stands will greet and supply you with trail information and small snacks.

Technology

One of the disadvantages of walking the planet is that you detach yourself from the convenience of technology.

People need technology in order to make their lives easier but the New World Pilgrimage movement is all about embracing a simple lifestyle and eliminates the need for technology. Cameras, personal computers, cars, or anything unnecessary because it takes time to produce and we want to free the people from things that take time to produce. Sticking strictly to food, shelter, and clothing liberates people. Because to have those devices somebody has to provide them. You enslave yourself and others the more you want and the more you think you may need.

Although convenient, technology tends to make us isolated. For instance, we use headsets to listen to our favorite tune when jogging, we use the computer to shop online instead of going to the supermarket, and we revel at the fact that we have thousands of friends in social networking sites but only a handful in real life.

The thing is that the world has gone upside down because we have relied so much on technology. The more advance our technology becomes, the more we become lazy and narrow-minded. Starting your journey and leaving behind your mp3 player or your tablet is very heartbreaking but once you start your journey without them, you end up opening your senses to enjoy the sights, sounds and even smell of the things that are around you. You will actually experience life.

You will realize that there is beauty around you and that shunning away from technology is something that you should have done in the beginning, but we were lured into time saving devices that only tied up more of our time.

The greater danger of technology are the weapons that are being developed these days. With microwave, sonic (high frequency sound), emp drones, weapons already a reality, we really have to seriously think about the laws, who's making them, and who's enforcing them. In the wrong hands you can control the world without the nuclear missiles. There are so many soft kill weapons in our time it's only a matter of time before someone uses them against common people to control and eliminate the populace in an unfavorable manner.

It's time to simplify things and take charge of how we want to live before it's pushed upon us in times of crisis. Walking the planet which is before us is the middle ground between all things. It creates the right degree of peace in the world.

Technology will eventually enslave us, you already see the signs all around you, so use the communications that are now in place while you still have a chance. Change the world. There has never been another time in history like our current time.

Don't let technology run the planet. When you look at technology in the future remember this formula. The higher cancels out the lower.

- Spirit above Flesh

- Flesh above Machine

Communication

Can you live for a few weeks or months without communicating with your boss? Probably yes. But what about not communicating with your family, friends and business contacts? You will probably think it is ludicrous not to live without communicating with people who mattered to you particularly your business contacts.

Starting on a journey to circumnavigate the planet will mean that you will have to drop all communication in order to complete your journey. This can be a very scary thing for many people. In your case, you might be asking yourself these questions "What if something happens to me? How will I get help?" You do not have to worry because the trails and routes of the New World Pilgrimage movement have a support network that assists you with your needs particularly your emergency needs.

You might not be able to communicate with your friends and family, but you can arrange to meet them at a certain location on a certain day.

Meeting people will widen your horizon because you will be pushed to communicate with other people whom you will encounter in your journey. You will also get to meet with the people who are behind the support network thus even if you cannot talk to your friends, you will have gained new ones in your journey instead.

Police would be found all along the routes to assist in emergencies and animal control.

Medicine

One of the concerns that many people have when it comes to starting their own long journey to navigate the earth is getting sick. Walking on foot for a long time can be tiring and it is very easy to feel fatigue after a long day on the trail. With no hospitals in sight, should you still go on this journey even if you might sacrifice your health?

The answer is a big yes. The thing is that you are not really sacrificing your health if you decide to walk the earth. In fact, you are doing your body a favor by giving it the exercise that it needs. You might feel sore after a few days of walking because this is your body's way of telling you that you haven't adapted to your new lifestyle yet but give yourself four days before you see improvements. In fact, many people who have already experienced walking on long distances can attest that after a few days of walking, their bodies return to normal—some even better than usual. Moreover, some also did not have a need to take pain killers because they became healthier after the end of their journey.

You can still take with you a portable first aid kit to provide immediate treatments on scrapes, wounds, sun burn or insect bites. Your first aid kit is an indispensable tool should you encounter emergency problems in the middle of your journey. Now what if you really need to seek medical attention and your first aid kit is not enough. There are infirmaries situated strategically along the trail. Moreover, you can also ask fellow pilgrims to notify the support system to help you with your emergency situation.

You might be encouraged to walk the planet by yourself but you are never alone when it comes to facing situations wherein you require medical help under the New World Pilgrimage movement.

Clothing

One of the heaviest bulks of a travel backpack is clothes. Now imagine if you plan to go on a journey for a long time. How many clothes should you bring to keep you comfortable and protected at the same time? You might think that you need to bring several changes of clothes all the time. How heavy your backpack must be!

Clothing is one of the concerns of many people who want to travel the planet. Should they bring a lot or just enough? The answer is that the New World Pilgrimage encourages people to travel light which means that you should restrict your clothing to just one— what you are wearing. Pilgrims will not need to carry much stuff when walking. The way stations (way zones) are not too far apart.

You will not be able to enjoy your journey if you carry a very heavy backpack full of clothes. Moreover, the support system of the New World Pilgrimage will be the one to provide you with the clean clothes that you need. Remember that the trail has way stations or comfort zones where you can get clothes should your current ones be worn out. Do you have to spend for new clothes? No. The clothes are provided for by the support network as their way of advance payment when their turn comes to walk the Earth.

Entertainment

Walking the entire time is a tiring feat and most people just want to relax by the end of the day. Entertainment can mean many things and it can include watching a movie or playing pool. If you have these in mind, then I must disappoint you that you cannot have these kinds of entertainment once you embark on a journey with the New World Pilgrimage movement.

Don't get me wrong here. You can still have entertainment after a long and tiring day of walking and you get them out of the most trivial things in life such as exchanging hellos to other travelers you will meet along the way, talking with local people about the region or watching the splendor of nature that is spread across your eyes.

These types of entertainments are simple but they are the ones that are truly remarkable and memorable. Now if you are still looking for more ways to entertain yourself, then you should continue with your travel until you reach the way stations wherein you and the people behind the support network can work together to organize your own entertainment. You can organize an art show, storytelling, forum or you can sing around the campfire to boost your spirits up. The best thing about this kind of entertaining is that it gets more fun If you lend your hand.

Transportation

The rule of thumb if you start circumnavigating the planet is to avoid transportation at all costs. This means that you have to walk along the way until you reach your destination. You will only be cheating yourself if you could ride cars or buses if you get tired. Moreover, you will not feel the essence of your journey if you keep on rely on land transportation. The thing is, you have to walk and if you feel tired, then rest for as long as you would like as long as you continue your journey on foot. This is especially true if your journey involves walking on connected land masses.

There will be no more cars. All autos will be destroyed and thrown into pits created just for them. Automobiles are the cause of 1 million deaths every year worldwide. This is a holocaust if you think about it. We know that 1 Million + people are going to die next year from the automobile and yet we continue to drive them around for our own convenience. This is more deaths than most any war on a yearly basis.

Railways, trucks, and ships will be used to transport the workforce, materials, and supplies only.

There will be rough spots if you start your long journey but take note that the difficulty of your trip is worth every step because you learn more things and meet new people so that you can become a better person not only for yourself but also for other people. Add to that the internal knowledge that can be cultivated.

Remember that with New World Pilgrimage, we avoid those things that are unnecessary in our life. Using transportation would entail setting up an industry just to keep the automobiles going. With the unnecessary things in life, it breeds competition and competition is a type of evil. So let us discard the unnecessary things in our lives so that in the end we remove the evils in our life too.

The more unnecessary things you want the more time it takes to produce them. You burden both yourself and those who would produce the object. The benefit of New World Pilgrimage is to free up peoples time. To be free from things and free from the production of the unnecessary.

~ o ~

Chapter 8: The Goal

I have decided to give this topic its very own chapter even though it's real short because of its impact and significant importance to the New World Pilgrimage movement.

This is the goal of the New World Pilgrimage in order to put order and peace in this new and borderless world:

- To live "without" is the aim.
- To free the mind and spirit for higher things.
- To have the least amount of burden.
- To work young and then be free while you are still able bodied.

A goal must rule (Not a person). The goal would create our living environment.

Freedom comes by walking. The stagnant stationary living of possession based societies will always create borders and war. Walk the earth!!!

Mass human migrations on foot will become the middle ground between all things. It will enable real progress for all people.

Expanding the concept of freedom for all peoples.

~ o ~

Chapter 9: End of the Old World

The world has to collectively decide to remove the powers that exist. There will be some injustice to the rich, but this is a new world. For New World Pilgrimage to get started about 80% of the world population has to agree that this is the right way to go. It has to be such a powerful force that it pushes the question past the tipping point. Every idea has this tipping point. It will come naturally when the new way becomes common knowledge. From there people will see that our historic models of human exchange don't really work in growing populations with national borderlines that create two factions: those who have and those who don't have. A world association can be put together, so that everyone can act simultaneously and in unison worldwide at the right moment. Tipping the scales of power and entering into a new era of freedom.

Once this happens the stages of education and work will be put into place. Once there are sufficient routes, way stations, and supplies then the real journey will begin. The transition into the nomadic world has to be by the people of the world, there cannot be on nation standing, so they can act in unison, When all possessions and national borders are removed in every corner of the world and the support system is set up people of a certain age will then be able to walk around the whole planet on foot and help others to do the same. This is more than monumental... this is freedom for all people.

A billion unarmed non-violent people worldwide just walking in and taking the power away from those who want to possess things, but rather than forcing the issue, I would recommend and invite the leaders of the world to come together and agree on this borderless world direction. Explaining the will of the people. Installing the goal and having all world leaders stand down and work towards moving all things towards the New World of Pilgrimage. This is a much better and more civilized way, so that the transition clean and good. There is always that sticky point in history which is known as the tipping point.

To get things started everyone will have their turn to work in the production and development of food, shelter, and clothing. Everything from growing crops, distribution, law enforcement, maintaining routes, building construction, demolition (of the old world), art, teaching, manufacturing clothes, manufacturing sea worthy ships, railways, and the destruction of all automobiles and demolition of old world structures that don't fit the new model of mass migration.

Everyone will also have their turn to see the world with all your basic necessities prepared for your journey.

The problem in today's direction is that as things become more and more efficient for the rich the less and less need there will be for people to work and have jobs, this is where riots and control would most likely happen. To control the situation they will limit your freedom. They will cause more barriers supposedly for your protection. It will be brought to you under the guise that is good for everyone. Even going to the extreme of creating events or allowing events to happen just to justify their laws of control, so why not change the system completely towards one that make sense where people are equal in a more natural way.

When you watch the news from now on, consider New World Pilgrimage and the five pillars of the new nomadic world society. By using the remarkable goal of New World Pilgrimage's earned citizenship, the walking around the planet on foot, and the helping of others to do the same, you will realize an amazing phenomenon. That it is just a matter of people joining together. No more living the great lies. Simply apply the 5 Pillars of New World Pilgrimage when you see your local or world news and you will know that it doesn't have to be this way. We can change it.

In the past nations needed weapons to defend themselves. Today with the advancement of communications mass numbers of people can be coordinated around the globe to rid the planet of those who want to keep us enslaved to possessions and property; bringing in a free new world for the people and by the people. Let's expand the great concepts of freedom for this journey of a lifetime.

~ o ~

Chapter 10: Freedom

"Then the LORD said to Moses, "Go to Pharaoh and say to him, 'This is what the LORD, the God of the Hebrews, says: "Let my people go, so that they may worship me."
-Exodus 9:1

Just as Moses said to Pharaoh to "let my people go", so to I say that the governments of the world must let the people go, drop their borders, and allow for the great exodus to come.

The Israelites wandered in the desert for 40 years and their troubles only really started when they settle and wanted a king, like the other nations.

If you plan on starting your own journey on foot, then the very thing that you will achieve with your first step is freedom. Freedom is such as broad word and this intangible word may mean a lot of things like freedom from oppression, re-establishing rights, civil liberty and autonomy. But how can the New World Pilgrimage help people achieve greater freedom?

First, let me ask you this question. What is freedom for you? What are the things that you consider a bondage to your personal growth and development? Is freedom for your ability to own things? Each individual, when asked this question would answer differently. For some, freedom is all about being able to live without having to worry about their finances. For some, freedom is to overcome their failures in life. So what is freedom for you?

I am not being rhetoric here but this philosophical question is merely asking you how you define the concept of freedom. By doing so, you will be able to find out how the New World Pilgrimage movement can help you achieve the kind of freedom that you are looking for. Below are the examples on how this movement can help you achieve your freedom.

- Freedom FROM technology. Whether you deny it or not, modern society is dependent from technology. Are you a person who always cringes when you see your boss' name on your incoming call? Are you also addicted to check your social networking accounts all the time? If yes, then you are definitely tied to technology. The New World Pilgrimage will force you to stay away from technology. It may be hard for you at first but you will find it liberating after being able to focus on your journey.

- Freedom FROM consumerism. Every day, we have to deal with the rising cost of commodities and it seems that we rely so much on money in order to be able to survive. There is more to life than money and the New World Pilgrimage teaches us that money cannot buy everything.

- Freedom FROM limitations. We limit ourselves from doing the best that we can be. Have you ever told yourself "I cannot do it"? If yes, then you are limiting your potential from succeeding in life. If you start with your journey, you will be able to push yourself and realize that you can do more than your limits. The self-determination to make it around the planet on foot.

- Freedom FROM cultural prejudice and traditions. Although beliefs and traditions are very important in forming our identities and ideologies, the problem is that it is our traditions and beliefs that prevent us from truly knowing and accepting other people. We stereotype other people because they don't fit our beliefs and norms and this causes misunderstanding and miscommunication. However, embracing the New World Pilgrimage movement allows you to cast aside your beliefs and traditions because you don't have to rely on your family, community, or nation support. Everything is provided for you. It is the unlearning of our beliefs and traditions according to where you're at in life and maybe building and re-enforcing those beliefs if you find them true. All this in a more tolerant world of the nomad. It's this that will set us free so that we may also see other people equally regardless of who they are.

~ o ~

Final Thoughts

The New World Pilgrimage movement is a novel idea that encourages everyone to walk this planet and be accountable with other people so that the movement will continue to flourish in perpetuity. Although there will be many who will doubt and fear this movement, it might take a while for those who support it to push the movement and encourage more people to get together.

The world is experiencing too much despair already and it seems that mankind has lost faith to humanity. What this movement needs to do is to show to the world that there is still some goodness left in people once we are free of the old world system that we currently live in and if we are successful in showing people what the New World Pilgrimage is all about, then it will be easier to convince other people to join. It might take 10, 50 or a hundred years of bringing this revelation forward, but we'll get there and when we do, the world will be a better place to live in.

I also hope that this book will be a nice springboard to start conversation and possible action towards a new method of thinking and action.

~ THE END ~

www.ingramcontent.com/pod-product-compliance
Lightning Source LLC
Chambersburg PA
CBHW060309290526
45789CB00001B/453